THE

EVANGELIST

THE

EVANGELIST

"A Story of Two Preachers"

Evangelist Mark Dunfee

Dedication

I dedicate this book to the preachers who came before. In white shirts and navy-blue suits, with narrow ties and sideways tie bars, they came. And to the godly women who preached under the anointing *the greatest story ever told.*

To cities and towns, with a Bible, a tambourine, and a bottle of oil, they came. These are the ones that changed the world.

I dedicate this book to every young person who has the call of God on their life. You are the last hope of the Earth. You are the candlesticks in the book of Revelation.

On the shoulders of giants of the faith who

came before, you now stand. You are precious to God, and you are precious to me.

> For the preaching of the cross is to them that perish foolishness; but unto us which are saved it is the power of God. (1 Corinthians 1:18)

> For after that in the wisdom of God the world by wisdom knew not God, it pleased God by the foolishness of preaching to save them that believe. (1 Corinthians 1:21)

Your friend,

Evangelist Mark Dunfee

Contents

1

The Man from the Sawdust Trail

In a little town outside of Austin, Texas, Melvin Brankard preached like a house on fire. His voice was raspy from fifty years of preaching revivals. Melvin's pants were a little short and his shiny suits were a little bit too tight. The hair on his head was combed straight back and was a little long, and probably a lot out of style.

Time had passed Evangelist Melvin by and the crowds weren't all that big. Most nights Melvin preached to wide, widowed women, and a few old men, and some scattered children. Mostly in churches that were on the wrong side of the tracks. Churches of yesteryear. Churches with old tattered songbooks that lay silent behind the old metal theater seats.

At night, worn carpets near the front of the churches he went to felt the weight of Bro. Melvin pacing back and forth. Wild gestures were made with wide, outstretched, flying arms.

To the unchurched, he looked scary. To the lukewarm, he was too loud. But for someone destroyed by the devil and going to hell, he was Heaven sent.

Oftentimes the messages were a little long and the points somewhat wandering. A cold theological seminary professor would have scoffed at his style of delivery. But Heaven noticed when Melvin preached. The itinerant old preacher was far more impressive to God than he was to man. Not that Evangelist Melvin cared. Melvin's back was straight and his words were straight. And every night his message was straight from God's Word: "Get saved or you will go to hell." No compromise. This evangelist had no soul searching about what people would think of him.

There was absolutely no depression for Evangelist Melvin Brankard. Only a full cup of soul satisfaction. A life lived in joy for the Master. Melvin had given God the strength of his youth and now God would give Melvin strength at the sunset of his ministry.

When Evangelist Melvin first heard the Call

into the ministry, pulpits were filled across the land with men of God like him. Now they were all gone. Like a tongue-talking dinosaur from another age, Evangelist Melvin still roamed the land. Could he have adapted? Yes. Could he have fit in a little bit more? Yes. But Evangelist Melvin didn't fit in with this world. He didn't want to. Melvin didn't care if he ever fit in.

Sometimes just before Bro. Melvin would preach for an hour, he would rear his head back and sing, "This world is not my home, I'm just a passing through, My treasures are laid up somewhere beyond the blue, The angels beckon me from Heaven's open door, And I can't feel at home in this world anymore."

The longer that Melvin lived, the less he felt at home in this old world. And sad to say, the less the world, and especially the church world, felt comfortable having Evangelist Melvin in to preach for a week. Most of his friends had gone to glory. But Bro. Melvin still preached and ministered in it every night.

In his heyday, Evangelist Melvin could command a crowd of hundreds of people every night. Sometimes a thousand or even more. He had been sought after as a campmeeting preacher all across the nation. Literally dozens of young preachers had heard the Call to preach in Melvin's meetings. Most of these preachers had forgotten him. God never had. Some of them were now professional clergy. Their lamps were going out.

A number of them felt that they had outgrown the same methods that saved them and their families from hell. Scared of a dip in the offerings and attendance, they were ashamed of the Gospel. Ashamed of what the Apostle Paul in the New Testament calls the foolishness of preaching (1 Corinthians 1:28). The method that God Himself chose to save the world. All the wood, hay, and stubble of their ministry would never survive the fire at the Judgment Seat of Christ. What Melvin had done for decades would last for eternity. And his work on Earth wasn't over yet.

The one who turned the water into wine still shows up. Just like when Jesus turned the water into wine at the wedding at Cana of Galilee, Jesus saved the best wine for last for Evangelist Melvin. It's worth it to stay true to God and God's calling on your life.

In the 21st century, the sawdust trail had pretty well vanished. So had the crowds and so had the offerings. With his friends mostly in

Heaven, it was a new era for Bro. Melvin and for the church. The time had come when men would not endure sound doctrine. The hearts of many had waxed cold. But Evangelist Melvin was still on fire. And God was going to use the fire within him to revive the world.

Bro. Melvin found grace in the eyes of the Lord. And because of that grace, great mercy would come upon the Earth. God never needs a crowd. Heaven never needs a majority. God still had a remnant. God still had Evangelist Melvin Brankard.

This evangelist just didn't fit in with a modern clergy that made sinners feel comfortable in church. Melvin never understood a contemporary style where the preaching of the cross had all but vanished, where the power of the Spirit had ceased to flow, and where no one got saved. No healings took place. No deliverance for the body and soul.

Now, in an old car pulling a silver trailer, Melvin pressed on preaching for those who would have him. But Melvin Brankard never preached for people. He preached for Jesus, whom he loved with all of his heart. It was a lifelong call. A commitment that would only cease when Jesus came back or when Melvin stopped breathing. One or the other would happen soon.

Though he labored now in the bayous and backwoods, Heaven embraced Melvin. Every night his angel and other ministering spirits would stand by with folded wings while Melvin preached salvation through the Jesus that Heaven adores. It was and is the Gospel. The power of God unto salvation. A message the angels have never been permitted to preach.

Yes, angels stood and watched in Melvin's meetings. They weren't always there at the beginning of the service. But the sound of what he was preaching and the worship would draw the heavenly angel band. They came because the spirit in those meetings reminded them of Heaven. And they wanted to help. They were like Melvin Brankard. They were on assignment.

Sometimes when Melvin preached, an angel would come and stand by his side. Unseen by the scattered few in the weeknight audience, the angel would wrap a heavenly arm around the old preacher. Melvin would feel what he called "a quickening from the Lord." Sometimes a heavenly hand would be placed on Evangelist Melvin's back, especially during the altar call.

In most churches, the altar call was a

historical relic of yesteryear. Melvin had one every service, and sometimes more than one. It was preaching that demanded a decision. It was God-breathed. It was eternal.

Angels often lined the walls of the country churches and mostly forgotten places where Melvin preached. The convicting power of the Holy Spirit came into these meetings. It was and is the life-changing power of God.

Often, toward the end of Melvin's God-given message, angels that lined the sides of the church would leave their places. They glided toward some wandering soul in the audience. The unseen angel would point them toward the altar. Then, if the sinner would come down front, the angel would walk the old hardwood floor aisle with them.

How the angelic company would rejoice in

the altars when Melvin would pray the Prayer of Salvation with even one little child. Then, in the glorious speed of celestial light, one or two of the angels would leave the service, instantly arriving in the heavenly City of Light to share the good report of what had just happened in Melvin's service. And then all of Heaven would rejoice. In fact, rejoicing would sweep across the angelic throngs in the city lighted by the Lamb.

Often, angel bands would race to a departed loved one in Heaven robed in white to tell them a backslidden child or a descendent had just repented in the old preacher's revival meeting. Melvin was mostly unknown on Earth but famous in Heaven for his faithfulness—and most of all, famous for his love for Jesus.

Everyone in Heaven knew of him and his exploits for God—things that mattered little on

Earth but set the heavens ringing. Yes, all of Heaven wanted to meet him. Melvin Brankard was a Hebrews chapter 11 saint, of whom the ecclesiastical world was unworthy. No, he never really did fit in. Bro. Melvin was just a passing through.

How the angels loved the old man. They had been sent by God on special assignment to stay with him. They were always near. Often in the corner of a cheap little motel room on the edge of town, the angels watched while Melvin slept. They wanted to take him home but they couldn't. His work was not done, but how they loved him because every night he lifted up the name of the one that they adore.

Evangelist Melvin was mostly ignored on Earth but surrounded by glory and talked about a lot in Heaven. Better to be unknown on Earth than to be unknown in Paradise.

2

The Performer

Evangelist Zach Whitman was everything that Melvin Brankard was not. Zach was handsome and articulate. A designer suit hung on Zach's shoulders just like it was supposed to. When Zach walked into a room, he looked like a European Prime Minister.

He walked like a somebody, talked like a

somebody, and looked like a somebody—somebody very prestigious and important. And, depending on your status in life, he could treat you like you were the most important person in the world or like a nobody. Mostly depending on if he wanted something from you. Everybody is somebody to Jesus. But not to Zach. Most people to Zach were invisible. Not even worth a second thought or a second glance.

Zach had several personalities. He could push an inner button and the personality he thought he needed would rise to perform. Public Zach and private Zach were not exactly identical twins. The handsome young evangelist had a hair-trigger temper, and woe unto the employee who crossed him.

He was sullen and moody when by himself. But Zach could be immediately transfigured by the red light on top of a TV camera. This personality could charm a snake or make a baby want to give him their bottle. Such was the power of his soulish man developed by years of practice and self-effort.

He was empty within yet glorious without. An absolute winner to the casual glance. This evangelist was a burning bush aflame with personality. But a burning bush that consumed itself. God's voice was not in the bush, only Zach's.

Tara, his wife of twenty years, didn't know who he was. Tara wasn't sure that even Zach knew who he was anymore. His kids didn't like him and he had no close friends. No one else was on his "anointed level." But the ground is level at the foot of the cross. No other fountain can cleanse us from all sin and unrighteousness. The rich and the powerful, the hurting and poor, all must come by way of the cross. Jesus said, "I am the way, the truth, and the life." (John 14:6). There is only one way to God. God is no respecter of persons. But Zach sure was.

What a self-presence the handsome young man had. When Zach walked into a room of people that were deemed worthy to impress, he came alive. And how he could work a room. The smooth in his voice was far beyond anything that a politician could ever dream of. But you can't politic the Lord. Heaven doesn't respond to charisma; it responds to faith and repentance and humility.

You can go far in the strength of the flesh. But it's a hard way. It's the "sweat of the brow" way (Genesis 3). It's no Garden of Eden of endless delights. And it's hard on your nerves and hard on your family. Zach was about to find out.

This exhausted man preached almost totally out of talent and not in the strength and anointing of the Holy Spirit. Actually, Zach didn't preach—he performed speeches about God. No demons trembled. They didn't fear him and barely knew his name. But they all knew and were scared of Melvin Brankard.

How these little imps of hell hated to go to one of Melvin Brankard's meetings to lie to someone. They always ended up trembling and running away or getting thrashed by an angel, especially when evangelist Melvin sang about the blood of Jesus and its power.

But no such things happened in the unseen world in Zach's meetings. Emotions were stirred, but oppressing spirits didn't have to leave. They walked in with people and they walked out with people. And none of them felt uncomfortable.

God wasn't an intimate friend with Zach anymore. He was spiritually deaf. He could no longer hear the Savior knocking on his heart's door, saying, "Let me in." Heaven seemed silent for the young man walking alone. And what a lonely walk it was. Without family and without friends. Worst of all, without peace.

It didn't have to be that way. It could have been different. It should have been different. It hadn't happened all at once either. It didn't happen fast. But now Zach felt like he was a million miles from God. It usually takes a long time for that to happen. But in a miracle-healing moment, you can get it all back. Zach would soon find out.

Zach was an echo and not a voice. A parrot and not a prophet. A broken vessel about to go to the Potter's House. Just in time. God's love and grace would find Zach when he couldn't find himself. When he couldn't save himself. Zach wasn't alone in that. None of us can save ourselves. All of us need a Savior.

This precious man preached behind a lonesome pulpit. When Zach preached, he preached alone. No heavenly arm embraced him. No angelic messengers left his services to go to a heavenly city. There was nothing to report. Nobody knew Zach Whitman in Heaven. But on Earth, Zach was highly esteemed among men. Always surrounded by people singing his praises.

What a delivery Zach had in giving a Gospel speech. Everything hummed. Whatever his writers put on paper Zach could perform. Zach could make people laugh. He could make them cry. Nobody was offended. Nobody was helped. But boy, did the self-help machine ever buzz.

Zach excelled in fundraising. Everything spun to the tune of tens of millions of dollars a year. But money wasn't the problem. Zach's heart was the problem. He performed professionally in the name of someone that he really didn't love.

Zach's soul was cold. And nobody seemed to know. The crowds didn't know. The preachers who tried to copy Zach didn't know. But Zach knew it. And Zach's wife knew. And Melvin Brankard whenever he saw Zach on television knew.

3

The Empty Preacher

Sometimes in a little motel room, "LIVE with ZACH WHITMAN" would come on in the room where Evangelist Melvin was staying. Bro. Melvin would put his hand on the TV screen and pray, "Jesus, help this young man. Don't let him be a castaway."

If Zach had gone to one of Bro. Melvin's

meetings, Zach would have pitied him. But Bro. Melvin pitied Zach. He pitied anyone who wasn't really close to the Lord, and that included preachers. That included Zach.

A form of godliness but denying the power of God is what Zach had (2 Timothy 3:5). It was all that he had and he didn't even know it. Being religious without a relationship with the Lord Jesus Christ is not pleasing to God. It can happen to anyone. It had happened to Zach. Superficial success was all that he had. It is never enough.

In the natural seen world Zach looked amazing. Anytime, anywhere, Zach's agency could book the biggest convention centers and draw hordes of people. But no angels walked the aisles drawing people to Jesus Christ. There was no flow of the Holy Spirit for them to operate in. No heavenly angelic security accompanied Zach to the huge auditoriums he was booked in. But an earthly security detail sure did. They talked in their unseen microphones and cleared the way for the Earth celebrity.

People would press against the ropes, hoping for an autograph. Just a glimpse of their star would bring cheers. But Heaven was not applauding the superstar's "Zach and Jesus Show" for the digital age. It was self-help and self-serving. The message was about man, by man, and man made to the core. But people couldn't seem to get enough of it. They loved it. And Zach Whitman loved being loved by the crowd. And being paid well for it.

He didn't want to be blessed to be a blessing. He was starting to love money. It was a scorecard and symbol. Money had him and he was poor on the inside. Some preachers had even more than Zach had but they used it to win souls. God wouldn't have cared how much money Zach had if he hadn't started worshipping it. Having money wasn't the problem; money having Zach was the problem.

The spirit of mammon affected every decision that he made. He was poor and naked in God's sight, though rich by man's standards. Evangelist Zach was basically printing money. But the amount of money coming in wasn't the problem. The fact that Zach was starting to love it was.

God wouldn't mind someone with faith bringing in a billion dollars if they loved and honored God and helped people. But prosperity is an even bigger test than poverty, and Zach didn't just have money, the money had him. It had dulled his soul. It was what he measured everything and everybody by, which was wrong.

Online and in line at the product table, people bought millions of dollars of merchandise. On satellite TV, Zach Whitman was a celebrity. It really looked like things couldn't be going any better. Zach had started out good and started out strong. But the idolatry of people had affected him.

He had pleased a lot of people, but he hadn't pleased the Lord. The praise of men is nectar that is quite addictive. Yes, when Zach Whitman preached, he preached alone with no heavenly assistance.

Sometimes while on the road late at night, in his suite a dim light could be found. But Zach was not up praying. The dim light came from a computer. People in some chat rooms would have been quite surprised to know who they were really talking to. It was sad. It was scary. It was sinful. If not for the prayers of the saints, Zach would have been totally shipwrecked.

Most of the believers who made the most difference didn't even know it. Their prayers had been prayed on time and in the Spirit. Those prayers of intercession worked. They sent goodness and mercy chasing after him—to save his soul and to save his ministry.

Zach's wife didn't travel with him much anymore. He was applauded in the press but not respected at home. She had her life and he had his. In fact, they hardly lived together. Only a big-time donor or photo shoots for advertisements made their worlds intersect. They used to fight like alley cats. Now it was the cold war. A marital permafrost as cold as Zach's prayer life.

An undercurrent so thick that you could cut it with a knife was always present.

Zach had started his ministry well, loving God and loving people, but now most of that was all gone. A million little compromises had soiled his soul. First, the compassion had left. Then the joy. And now the peace. But the show must go on.

Zach's schedule was booked three to four years ahead of time by professional handlers. Evangelist Zach didn't pray about where to go. Direct mail response and the demographics of a city told him where to go. Zach was not guided by the Holy Spirit; he was guided by a computer analytics program run by people who weren't even saved. They projected where he could get the most money and biggest crowds. No leading of the Holy Spirit. Strictly big business. There is nothing wrong with structure and being organized, but when you haven't listened to the still small voice of the Holy Spirit in years, something is desperately wrong.

Often, at night after a huge meeting, Zach would silently sip a glass of wine on his private plane. It was handed to him by the female attendant. As he looked out the window, he would think about what a success the meeting had been. Zach was thinking about the crowds and the receipts—about the bulging database of new partners.

Unfortunately, no one in Heaven was talking about the meetings where Zach performed for the masses. And the hole in Zach's soul was growing. Growing bigger and emptier every day. It was almost getting a little hard for the studio makeup pros on the set to cover up the growing darkness within. Zach could see it when he looked into the mirror. His wife could see it. And Evangelist Melvin could see it whenever he saw Zach on Christian TV.

Zach was starting to think about a whole lot more than Jesus while on the road. Even though his wife abhorred her, he had a 25-year-old whiz-kid female assistant who "actually understood him." It was a lot more fun to be constantly idolized by a young blonde in a tight skirt than to listen to his wife complain all the time.

He hadn't been to bed with this young lady, but she was sure on the top of the list just in case sometime things didn't work out with his wife, Tara. Zach had silently reached out through one of his most trusted associates to a couple of other major ministry leaders that had traded in their wives. He wanted to know: How did it affect the direct mail base? What was the lag time on a ministry recovery?

Lust was a radiation in his bones. It had been pretty well kept and undercover. After all, didn't everyone have their "problems"? But this was just the physical lust; the lust of the eyes—to succeed and be a *big-time* success—was all-consuming.

Whatever it took, Zach would do it. No hours of work were too long. No burden too great to bear. All in the name of Jesus for the glory of Zach. He had been to the mountaintop and seen all the ministry kingdoms that others had, and Zach was ready to bow to whoever and whatever to get one.

God's favor and grace hadn't built Zach's ministry. Zach had—by the sweat of his brow and the strength of his flesh. And that is exactly what it took to keep the ministry going. That which is born of the flesh is flesh, and that which is born of the Spirit is spirit (John 3:6).

Zach Whitman's sin was not a jet; lots of godly ministers have jets. His sin was not fundraising; many fine ministries raised even more money than he had and used it all for God's glory. Zach's sin was pride and becoming lukewarm. He had left his first love. What started out as all about Jesus was now all about him.

The ministry mask he wore on his face all day long was now permanently glued to his face. So glued and attached that he couldn't even see himself when he looked into the mirror at night. He was a stranger to his family and to himself. Zach was an actor playing a part—the part of an evangelist. You can fool people but you can't fool

God. And you can't fool yourself forever.

Zach had lost his inner compass. Daily adjustments in the secret place are what keep us on track. The candle of the Lord had nearly gone out. Zach's platform presence had become stagecraft. Like an Old Testament King Saul, he labored on. But without a prayer life, Zach struggled to emotionally stay afloat.

Most all of his books on revelation knowledge were ghostwritten. It had started out occasionally, but now most of his sermon material was also ghostwritten. It sure wasn't Holy Ghost written. Quite a radical departure for someone who used to listen every day for the still small voice. Now Heaven was silent. It couldn't be heard above the busy hustle and bustle of the streetcar called Success.

Sometimes a depression of fear so deep that

he could hardly breathe would come on Zach at around 3 o'clock in the morning. But just like a good Hollywood actor, Zach kept performing. Zach played the part. It was an Oscar-winning performance. Sadly no one noticed. The crowds just kept getting bigger. The invitations to appear kept pouring in.

Where had he missed it? Where had he actually gone off track? The Lord would have gladly shown him. But Zach was so busy "working for God" that he didn't have time for God.

Zach hadn't actually committed adultery, but the "What ifs" and the "What would it be like?" doorbell constantly rang in his mind. No wonder Zach's wife, Tara, no longer traveled with him. The short skirts and low-cut blouses of those who worked at ministry headquarters were very distressing to Tara. Their marriage was a train wreck waiting to happen. Tara had gotten tired of complaining and now had given in to a deep spirit of despair.

Tara remembered when she and Zach had started preaching after Bible school. With a humble little four-cylinder car, they went to tiny little out-of-the-way places before they "made it big." Back then they were praying people surrounded by praying people. Now they were managed by worldly consultants and advisors.

At one time, Zach and Tara had been Spirit-filled and Spirit-led. Now they didn't pray together, sleep together, eat together, or hardly even live together. They had even started thinking and saying that this was just the price you pay for success. But somewhere deep in Zach's heart, he knew it was the price you pay for loving the praise of men more than the approval of God. Now all they had was a hollow business ministry arrangement.

Zach looked with disdain at anyone beneath his elite level as a national ministry. As an A-list Christian celebrity, he could name his price for any appearance. If someone didn't like it, so what? The line was backed up with people who would. Places that were more than willing to oblige each and every demand. But the meticulous image that Zach cultivated nationally didn't measure up with what he was at home.

Zach's ministry didn't extend to the gated community where he lived. In his home, where his ministry should have been the strongest, it was the weakest. Now it was harvest time at home where he lived.

4

The Remembered Book

fter midnight in the wee hours of a
Saturday morning, Zach's pilot landed
the ministry jet at a private airport. It was not far
from the gated community the Whitmans called
home.

It actually was just a house. A real big house.
A magnificent house doesn't make a home. It

hadn't been a home in many years. Maybe never had been a home. But it wasn't the devil's fault. It was Zach's fault. God made Zach the head of the home and Zach had failed. Failed to love, failed to pray, and failed in the ministry that he should have loved the most: his family.

So, now what he had was a launch pad and a landing place; an ornate structure that was built upon the sand. Happiness didn't live there and never had. But strife sure did. Although not for much longer because it was about to be asked to leave... with the help of the police if necessary.

After being driven by staff members to his house, Zach noticed the lights were on in his library. "Was Tara still up?" he wondered. He went inside, barely noticing that she was standing by the fireplace.

"Zach, we need to talk," she said.

Already exhausted and irritable from an eighteen-hour, pressure-packed day, Zach said, somewhat sarcastically, "Can't it wait?" shrugging her off and starting to head for his own room. Ignoring her was his standard way of dealing with his wife. But she made it clear that wasn't going to work so well tonight.

"No. It can't wait... because I'm leaving you," Tara replied. "And you will be the one moving out. But whatever you do, don't wake up the children. Go into one of your rages and I'll have the cops here in five minutes. I already have an attorney. Give me a hard time and I'll have him send a prepared press release to the paper immediately.

"Zach," Tara continued, "You are not the man that I thought I was marrying years ago. I'm tired of seeing someone on TV that I don't even know. I wish I had a man of God for a husband, not just someone who pretends to be a man of God when the camera is on."

Zach could feel angry words coming up in the back of his throat and an almost primal urge to yell. But somehow, he kept his mouth shut.

Tara was not a preacher, but she sure was preaching that night—to a congregation of one. "I feel sorry for you, and I really don't know if I've ever met a more miserable person," she said with an almost pitiful look on her face that was puffy from crying. "I'm not saying we have to divorce, but that is probably the direction things are going. I want you out of here in the morning, so, either God does something quick or I will see you in court." Then Tara turned and walked upstairs.

As sick as it sounds, Zach's first thoughts were a financial tally of his assets. And there was a quick mental roll call of other ministers who had survived such a personal crisis. Then he almost felt a sense of relief. Their marriage, after all, had died a slow, excruciating death a long time ago. Maybe this was an opportunity.

Incredibly, out of pride and stupidity, Zach almost called his twenty-five-year-old blonde assistant just to talk, of course. Thank God he didn't.

Any number of godly pastors would have talked to him and prayed with him and given him advice, even at that hour of the night. But Zach didn't call. The godly relationships with other men that the Lord would have put in his life just were not there. They could have been. But friends didn't matter to Zach. This evangelist didn't view people as friends. He viewed them as competitors. And Zach didn't take advice; he only gave advice.

No doubt his publicist could make a statement. Zach could blame it on the devil. The public, after all, has a pretty short attention span. The thought processes of a totally carnal mind like Zach had could be pretty strange. But even showmen have limits. And even hard-hearted men have feelings.

Inside, Zach started to ache. His breathing got funny and a sadness descended on him that was almost suffocating. Empty eyes advertised the empty soul within. Then, like a mechanical toy whose batteries were wearing out, Zach trudged to his largely ceremonial library.

As Zach sat alone in his beautiful study, he thought about how little time he spent there.

Once in a while, to impress someone, he met them there for a meeting, or sometimes to sign important papers. But that was it.

In the early days, Zach hadn't even had an office. He would go alone into old Sunday School classrooms in the churches where he ministered. With his Bible, books, legal pad, and an old briefcase, divine business was transacted. Heaven spoke. Now, in this presidential-like study, Heaven was silent. The saddest part was that Zach had never even noticed.

Now, Zach was silent too. Just staring out the window at the manicured lawn dimly lit by the glowing security lights outside. With no friends and no one he trusted that he could call, Zach just sat there with angry thoughts, too proud to pray. He was wounded within even worse than he knew. That's what the devil and pride do to people. One day they wake up empty and a broken shell of what they used to be.

So, Zach sat alone in the dark and was a living and breathing exhibit A of "to whom much is given, from him much will be required." (Luke 12:48). The handsome young evangelist had been, thus far, a losing investment for Heaven. But God doesn't broker and sell His losing investments. The Lord keeps loving them and reaching out to them, trying to get them to repent—even preachers gone bad, in a beautiful library, sitting alone in the dark.

Sometimes it takes a long time to get lukewarm. Then it takes quite a while longer to grow cold. But when you get there, the world gets loud and Heaven gets quiet. And after a while, the voice of Heaven just seems to stop. When the silence comes, repentance is about the only thing that will bring it back. Repentance or someone praying for you.

Behind Zach's mahogany desk were some shelves in a prestigious looking cabinet with glass doors. A cabinet that almost looked like something in a judge's chamber. To the un-trained eye, you would never even notice, but on the lower middle shelf were a few books that at one time, many years ago, were Zach's favorites.

Once upon a time, they really meant a lot to him. They were mostly paperbacks. Some had the worn covers taped on. The books were well traveled. In the early years, they went with Zach and Tara in a little four-cylinder car across America. Most of the books in Zach's prestigious study had never even been read. They were there just for looks. Just for show. But these books were different.

Every page of these little books tucked away on the middle shelf had been read, marked, and highlighted. Some had been cried on. Yet it had been about ten lonely years for the books since they had seen their evangelist friend. But they still had power in their pages because they had been written by Holy Ghost men of God.

Doing what these men of God taught him had launched his ministry. They taught him the Word of God. Not doing what they taught had led Zach to an awful place. A temporal place of vanity and vexation of spirit.

As a young man, he had learned about the eternal but slowly abandoned it. Nothing eternal had happened in Zach's office for years and years. But somehow, in the early dawn, Zach was drawn to the lower middle bookshelf.

Only Heaven knew why his empty, weary

eyes with bags under them went to those few books—to one in particular. Zach had read that one so many times as a young man that it was almost memorized. But it hadn't been touched in over a decade. A sad, silent decade for Zach hearing God's voice.

Now embalmed on a bookshelf, it had once been his favorite book. A book that made him cry, pray, and love souls. His old Thompson Chain Reference Bible and this book were his most important tools. He used to reach for them in the morning. They traveled with him all during the day and then sat by his bedside at night. The tattered old cover was so familiar. Yes, his Bible and this book changed his whole life.

In the dark library, in the middle of the night, *grace* nudged Zach. Not a hard shove.

Grace isn't like that. Just a gentle touch. But hard enough that something wonderful happened to the broken evangelist.

Zach didn't even know why, but a desire to pick up that little paperback book came on him—came on him softly and tenderly, and would not let him go. Zach didn't deserve it, but that's the way grace is. For all of us.

Grace makes all the difference.

For some reason, Zach put that tattered old friend of a book in his Italian leather, custom-made attaché case. Right now, it was about the only friend that Zach had. Except for the author of the book, which grace was about to engineer for Zach to meet.

In fact, that meeting had been planned since the foundations of the world. That's the way God works. That's the way grace is. God doesn't give up on us when we have fallen and when we have lost our way. Jesus loves broken people even when it looks like they can't ever be put back together again. God even loves broken preachers. Maybe especially broken preachers who have been broken in battle and look like they will never rise again.

God doesn't give up on anybody. He is not willing that any should perish but that all should come to a saving knowledge of the Lord Jesus Christ (2 Peter 3:9). Resurrection power can make anybody rise again. Zach would soon find out.

And with that, Zach picked up the tattered old paperback book. It was titled, "HOW TO HEAR THE VOICE OF GOD" by EVANGELIST M. L. BRANKARD.

5

Alone in Luxury

With an Italian leather attaché case full of truth, Zach still had a phone call to make before he headed out the door. It was never too late for him to call his general manager. Middle of the night phone calls were not uncommon.

A designated cell phone with a special

ringtone for Zach was always with the ministry's GM. It might not ring for days, or it might ring every five minutes for several hours. But when the phone rang, it had best not go to voicemail. Zach might be unavailable for days on end, but when he called you, he expected prompt obedience and attention.

Only Zach had this phone number, but any one of five Zach Whitman personalities could dial it. The GM never knew which one would be on the other end of the line. Zach was not filled with the Fruit of the Spirit. He ran on pure adrenaline and raw emotion. And it sure showed. Unfortunately for everyone around him, it sure made for some high highs and some low lows.

Zach was not much of an emailer. He was a talker and couldn't care less about inconveniencing anybody who worked for him. With the compassion of an Egyptian taskmaster in the Old Testament, Zach pushed himself and his people hard. In his own words: "That's why I pay you the big bucks."

Sneering sarcasm was one of his favorite weapons to lead. If you didn't like it, quit. They would hire someone else tomorrow. He who needed so much mercy was not very quick to hand it out. Zach had been that way for years, and it did not please the Lord. It didn't please anybody else either. But Zach really only wanted to please Zach. He had been that way for years. Anyone who worked for him sure earned everything that they got.

So, in the middle of the night, the dreaded phone rang by the general manager's bed. The GM answered it before the second ring. No pleasantries were exchanged. It was all business. And Zach was in an especially foul mood.

Soon into the call, the young evangelist barked, "Handle it!" into the phone at his general manager. A couple of employee situations in key positions, along with renewal contracts for media outlets needed attention.

When Zach was troubled, he could often do the work of ten men in a few days. At other times, Zach would zone out. He'd kind of disappear right off the radar for a few days. Then reappear and micromanage again. And woe to the employee who had made a mistake while Zach had been away on the mountain top or down in the valley. Zach had been known to fire people on the spot. But it's hard to fire yourself. Especially when you have become cold and hard.

Finally, Zach said, "Call the car service and tell them to be here in half an hour. Call for another car and have them pick up the suitcase that I always keep packed at the ministry; I need it tonight and I need it now. I also need the plane refueled, and make reservations for me at the Four Seasons in Austin. I want one of their best suites.

"Also," Zach continued, "Tell the people at the airport that I want a salad, along with the special dressing that I always get. Also, have them give me three kinds of fruit. And enclose the tally sheet with the most recent mail count and giving totals. Fed-Ex anything else that needs my immediate attention or that I need to sign. Try not to screw this up, okay?" And with that, Zach hung up the phone.

In the middle of the night, as Tara tossed

and turned and cried in her room, Zach soon walked out of the unhappy house. But he couldn't leave his unhappy self behind because years ago he had walked out on God.

As the car service dropped him off at the airport, Zach was stone-faced. Well, really it was his heart that was made of stone. When something happened that he didn't like or couldn't control, Zach just kind of zoned out. Like a magnet that had lost its power, Zach's weak inner man drifted. It was just the opposite of the Apostle Paul's confession, "Though our outward man perish, yet the inward man is renewed day by day" (2 Corinthians 4:16 KJV).

Zach's outer man actually looked pretty good. He worked out. Stayed away from too many carbohydrates after noontime. Zach always kept his hair cut just right. After all, he wanted to look good on TV. But for years, it had been way too much about the outside. On the outside, his ministry seemed so successful. So did his family. But inside, there was no peace. No joy. And now his soul, like a burning nuclear reactor core, continued to melt.

Tonight, nothing seemed to put out the fire. Repentance would have. Humility would have. But instead, Zach kept ignoring that there was something deep inside himself that needed to be fixed. Sometimes Zach would blame the devil. Sometimes Zach would blame Tara, or his childhood, or other people. But certainly never himself. His ego was too large for that.

In the eyes of people, he was an important man. A spiritual man. But the Zach Whitman who took flight in the middle of that night was an empty man. As the jet pointed to the sky, a backslidden preacher on it ate salad and sipped Perrier water. Then flirted with a young flight attendant, never thinking about it, or even realizing that the Spirit of the Lord had departed from him.

The private plane landed in Austin, Texas, and a car service was already there waiting just past the entrance, near the charter jet executive building. After a short ride, the chauffeured car pulled up to a back entrance of the hotel. He stepped onto the marble floor of a private elevator and soon was alone in his beautiful accommodations.

There were three magnificent bedrooms with French antique beds and matching high-end furniture. The ornate living room had a beautiful fireplace styled after the Élysée Palace in France. There was also a full kitchen with a 24-

hour-a-day on-call chef who would cook anything a person wanted for a meal. But the
exquisite antique French bed in the master suite
gave no rest to the weary preacher.

Sleep would not come. All that early morning and next day, Zach watched sports—any
kind of sports—read the New York Times, the
Wall Street Journal, and paced. Kind of like a lion
in a very luxurious cage, he walked around the
diamond suite of his hotel.

Zach wanted to go downstairs but he would
probably be recognized by somebody. Today
Zach was in no mood to say, "Bless you, brother"
to anybody. The very last thing he wanted to do
was to listen to someone's stupid problems, even
if it was just for a minute.

Sleep wouldn't come, so Zach found sleep in
a bottle. Not in a bottle of liquor but in a bottle of

sleeping pills. In a back compartment of a Ralph Lauren suitcase, he found them. Zach used to use them only on overseas trips. It helped him adjust to time zone changes. When you have to speak on success and always be up emotionally, you must have sleep, any way that you can get it. You have to be on your game. And you can't have too many circles under your eyes. At least not too many for a good makeup man to fix before going on live TV.

Zach took two sleeping pills and a couple of sips of Perrier water and the sandman started to come. The rich oak paneling on the walls started to come toward him. And someone else came too: the angel of the Lord. Sent by grace, a ministering spirit who had come to help Jesus save a preacher who had lost his way. All because someone somewhere prayed.

6

A Signpost from Heaven

Zach lay crossways the king-sized bed for several hours of medicated rest. He was also crossways with God, with his wife, Tara, and with the Call of God. When morning came for Zach, the world didn't know it. It was 1:00 a.m. Zach had been sleeping though sort of awake, and now he was awake but sort of sleeping. Sideways living isn't easy. There is no peace. No joy.

Earlier all that day, consultants had roamed the halls of Zach Whitman Ministries. Hired guns that would have been just as happy to work for Exxon or a direct marketing company. Whoever was the highest bidder got them. And everything that they saw was through a worldly lens.

Most of the spiritual people of prayer that helped launch Zach were long gone. Zach told himself that he had outgrown them—that they couldn't grasp the inner workings of a national ministry. Anyway, they were gone and Zach was left. Left sleeping sideways, tossing and turning on an oak poster bed.

Zach was a star. He was a take-charge kind of guy. A fixer. A mover of men. But Zach was driven and frustrated. Lonely and empty. And the only way to shut things down for a few hours was a sleeping pill that you swallow.

Years ago, Zach used to sleep like a baby with Tara's arms around him. He never went to bed without a Bible and a legal pad beside his bed. Often, he would wake up and pray, writing down things that the Holy Spirit spoke to him about. He had been close to the Lord and close to his soulmate, Tara. No more.

Worldly men talked strategy with him for hours at a time. Yet it had been years since he heard the still small voice in the night. When God spoke, no one was listening. At least Zach wasn't.

Zach was really alone. Many men of God never travel alone. Zach did. And it made him vulnerable and lonely. It was a mistake. One of many in his life.

Now wide-awake, Zach decided to leave the confines of his hotel room and go out onto the street. It might help him unwind, and a little exercise might do him good. It was the middle of the night, so Zach decided to go out the main entrance of the hotel.

Walking through the fabulous lobby, Zach almost stopped. He almost stopped at the bar. When you are lukewarm and worldly within, the flesh can find a lot of quick fixes. Maybe he could have an interesting conversation with someone while at the bar, he thought to himself.

It's not good for restless people to be alone. But Zach was. That was his choice. And choices have consequences for a family and for a pastor or evangelist and their ministry.

Somehow, the mercy of God kept Zach walking. Walking out into the moonlight, down empty sidewalk after empty sidewalk. Mercy kept him still walking even when a warm rain shower began. And then it happened.

Zach Whitman started to cry.

"Is it my nerves?" Zach thought. "Or am I losing it?"

It was a little more than a whimper and something less than a sob. A strong cough and his hand in front of his face would have covered it up had he seen someone. But there was no one to see him walking the empty streets all alone. So, the steady rain of tears kept falling.

Then, like a little breeze, Zach sensed it. Something settling upon him. A quickening within like a holy whisper. A breath of God from the presence of the Lord. And Zach sensed peace. The edge of the pressure lifted, and Zach sensed something pure and holy stirring him deep within.

Countless times he had yielded to the presence of the Holy Spirit through the years. That presence had revealed the Word to Zach, led him to Tara, and given him divine favor since his youth.

God doesn't give up on preachers when they are in trouble and don't even know it, and when deep within they have given up on themselves. So, crying on a street corner in the rain, Zach Whitman saw something that would forever change his life.

It was something that would change his ministry and populate Heaven because of what he would someday preach. It didn't look like much. In fact, thousands of people had walked on this street all day and no one even noticed. But destiny came.

Destiny never comes alone. Destiny always comes with grace. And grace caused Zach to look up and see a sun-faded poster advertisement. It simply said:

REVIVAL SERVICES ALL THIS WEEK

Revival services with M. L. Brankard at
Temple of the Living God.

7

The Midweek Service That
Changed the World

The following evening, when Zach gave his car service driver the address to the church, the man cursed and said, "What are you, nuts? Going to that side of town?"

But Zach said, "That's where I'm going and so are you. And you're going to wait for me. Just put it on my tab. And you best be there when I come out. I give this company a lot of business, so quit talking and drive."

If not for that speech, the driver would have squealed the tires and left the church yard immediately after Zach got out the car door. But stay he did. The driver never again would see the man that he dropped off. Neither would anyone else.

The driver had to stay parked outside the church a mighty lot longer than he ever planned. A whole lot longer than Zach ever planned too. God and Melvin Brankard never rushed.

Yes, the limo driver dropped one man off and would pick another man up later on. Same last name but a different man. Both of them named Zach. But their faces and hearts wouldn't look the same. Same outfit on both, but the clothes on the one coming out would look quite wrinkled. And would smell like olive oil. The old Zach that got dropped off would never, ever be heard from again. That's what God could do in just one service with Evangelist Melvin Brankard.

Zach Whitman really tried to not stand out as he walked into Temple of the Living God. A little, nondescript clapboard church where people still prayed. On the wrong side of the tracks but on the right side of faith.

Zach had on Gucci jeans, a twelve-hundred-dollar pair of alligator hide cowboy boots, a tailor-made shirt, and over that was a seven-hundred-dollar jacket, coupled with designer sunglasses on his head. Zach stood out. Really stood out.

A humble elderly usher met Zach at the

door. His name was Bro. Evans. He had on a faded purple suit with industrial black shoes and white socks. He warmly opened the door for Zach. The usher wasn't dressed for success but he pleased the Lord.

If both of them had dropped dead at the doorstep of the church, the old man Bro. Evans would have received far more reward in Heaven than Zach. He had done what he could. Zach never had.

God's yoke is easy. His burden is light. But God wants you to do your best with what He gives you to work with. The precious old man in the purple suit had always done that.

This elderly usher loved God. The saint did what God asked him to do, humble though it was. And Heaven noticed. In fact, he was famous in Heaven. But on Earth, nobody knew his name. Most of the people in the little church just sort of took him for granted.

So, a famous man opened the door for a man nobody knew—in Heaven. But the famous on Earth Zach barely looked sideways at the usher, except to glance at the man's silver tie bar and think, "I haven't seen one of those since I was a kid." Zach was going to see quite a few things that night that he hadn't seen since he was a kid.

Yes, it's really hard to stay under the radar in a weeknight church crowd of thirty-five people (a service that would change the world). And it was impossible to stay under the Holy Ghost radar that was flowing in that church that night.

Melvin Brankard was on a side bench, sitting and preparing his pure heart just before the service. He was "meditating in the Spirit" as he called it; getting the mind of the Lord.

His left arm was crossed and holding onto his elbow, with the palm of his right hand cradling the right side of his face. When Zach walked in, Bro. Melvin kind of jerked backwards as he sensed something change in the spirit. In all this though, his eyes were still closed. He was a Seer. A man of God. And there weren't many left. That's the way Bro. Melvin was.

When Bro. Melvin opened his eyes, he saw Zach. He recognized him in the natural, but his eyes looked right through him. Melvin didn't judge anyone by the flesh. He knew them in the spirit. And Bro. Melvin felt sorry for Zach and had compassion on him.

Well, at the same time Bro. Zach was having his own thoughts. He always had them. Humanistic thoughts that came from the mind of the flesh. It's one thing to get a touch from God on a sidewalk; it's another to have your mind renewed.

Zach's mind was not renewed. And the enemy did not want him there. So, thoughts like, "Why haven't they shut this church down?" bombarded Zach's mind. "Now, this is why I don't preach in churches anymore but control my own meetings," Zach thought. And that was his problem. He always wanted to be in control.

The local pastor stood up to start the service and immediately went into full preacher voice. The pastor hollered in a high shrill voice, "We welcome the saints of the Most High to the house of God here tonight! Going to be a meeting here tonight! Can you all say 'Amen!?'" And Zach wanted to leave.

He started to leave. His fleshly man knew he

had to leave. Zach stood up and headed out the door in his mind many times, but he simply couldn't. Something made him stay. Destiny had seemingly tied him to an old metal theater seat with a duct-taped patch on the brown padding. As hard as he tried to leave, he stayed. Seemingly every time he was about ready to get up, he decided to give it a few minutes more. There was a definite reason, and it was because people prayed.

In Missouri, a woman named Sis. Vera Devon abruptly took her apron off and said to her husband, "OK, you go ahead and finish supper. I'll clear the supper dishes away later. I have to pray and I have to pray right now."

Sis. Devon had never heard of Zach Whitman. She had never heard of Melvin Brankard. Sis. Devon was almost a thousand miles away from Austin, Texas when a spirit of intercession came on her so strongly that everything else had to cease.

In a farmhouse bedroom, next to a quilted bed, tears of intercession fell in the "strong name of Jesus." A woman unknown on Earth but celebrated in Heaven. That's why Zach tried in vain to leave the meeting but had to stay. Because Sis. Devon prayed.

There were others also. Audubato Mufumbo, during his morning prayer in Lomé, Togo, West Africa suddenly sensed his dialect change to a heavenly tongue that he had never heard or learned. The anointing of the Holy Spirit just kept surging and surging through him in heavenly currents. Also, one person in Ireland, two in Russia, and a teenager in California with headphones on listening to worship music.

The Holy Spirit tried to get others to also intercede. Some thought it was just them. Others fell asleep. But enough people prayed enough to keep Zach Whitman in an old theater seat. A seat with duct tape on it.

Enough prayed to also put a supernatural flow into the worship service at Temple of the Living God. And the saints prayed more than enough so that Melvin Brankard could preach a breakthrough message, then demonstrate in the power of the Holy Ghost. It happened because people around the world prayed in the Spirit.

That service would someday affect a few hundred million people. It happened on a summer's night in a midweek revival service with thirty-five people. Enough people prayed to change Zach Whitman's life.

When the saints prayed, the very atmosphere of the service changed. It was because people unknown did what was unseen to men. But Heaven saw and Heaven heard. Their prayers ascended like wisps of smoke into a holy place in Heaven. Then the heavenly host came. Came to a simple, plain, white clapboard church where people still prayed.

8

The Laying on of Hands

As the music started, Zach thought something was in his eye. There *was* something in his eye and it was a tear that desperately wanted to roll down his cheek. "What is this? These pitiful musicians couldn't play at a barn dance," Zach thought to himself. But something got on him when they played. It was called conviction and he hadn't sensed it in a long time.

He did now.

You see, Zach was used to Gospel entertainment by his professional band. They were gifted and talented, but superficial, not anointed, and unsaved. Most of them were good people, but they were playing for self-glory and not for the glory of God. The church mother's band was a lot different. They were anointed. Zach could hardly blink away the tears fast enough so that they didn't run down his face.

There was an old church saint with silver hair named Sis. Norma James leading song service. Sis. James, the song leader, was backed up by an upright piano slightly out of tune and a Gibson guitar with cheap strings. Right behind Sis. James, slightly to the right, sat a grey-haired saint playing the accordion. These ladies loved the Lord and played out of devotion to God.

That was more than could be said for Zach's high-priced band.

The accordion was an instrument of yester-year that used to be as common in churches as songbooks. The little white-haired woman played the accordion while it rested on a towel draped over her legs for modesty's sake. She played slightly out of rhythm and a little out of step with the nearby Gibson electric guitar which had a broken string. And she was backed up by the prayers of the saints.

What looked like a nursing home band was melting Zach's cold heart. It made no sense in the natural. But that's what happens when people pray. Zach Whitman was torn between looking at the pitiful musicians in the natural and what he was sensing in the supernatural.

Except for on the street corner, he hadn't

sensed anything in the supernatural world for a very long time, and he wasn't used to it. But he liked it. Why wouldn't anybody like it? And the more he sensed it, the more that he liked it.

Pastors that quench the Spirit literally stop the ability of God to deliver and set people free in their services, especially from any kind of bondage. That's why it's hard to be delivered in a lot of churches today. A form of godliness denying the power of God has never really set anyone free and never will. But in this church, it was different.

The sweet music flowed in wave after wave of glory over him. It swept right through him. It came deeper and wider. A flood of the glory of God. Something in that service would stay with Zach the rest of his life. It was the manifest presence of the Lord preparing people's hearts for the Word. The next two and a half hours were almost like a fog to Zach. But the fog would lift and Zach Whitman and his world would never ever be the same.

When Melvin Brankard got up to preach, there were no hollow platitudes about the famous Zach. Only bragging on Jesus. Jesus and Jesus in you was the only thing that impressed Melvin Brankard.

That very night 5,000 churches—many of them mega churches—would have craved having Zach Whitman come to a service. He could have named his price. But here in this midweek revival service, Evangelist Melvin Brankard never even mentioned his name, even though Zach was a "Christian celebrity." The only celebrity of this meeting was the Lord Jesus Christ. JESUS, crucified, risen, and SOON coming again.

Holding the old microphone with a cord on it like an old mini garden hose, Evangelist Melvin reared back his head to sing. With a husky voice, in the key of F, he sang, "Someday my time on Earth will be over, Someday my work will be done, Then I will go on to meet Him, In the land far beyond the sun."

And it was then that something so *strong* yet something so gentle, like a heavenly vice grip began to wrap around Zach's soul. And it would not let him go, because God doesn't let us go. Even when we have miserably failed, even when we are so full of self and have sinned.

The old evangelist preached for an hour and fifteen minutes. The message was "Is Your Lamp Full and Burning?" Sometimes the old man would tilt his head back slightly and give a shout. It wasn't just noise. It changed the very atmosphere. It brought angels. God inhabits the praises of his people. God inhabits this kind of praise.

There used to be a lot of shouting in a lot of churches. Not so much anymore. The Methodists used to do it. So did the Pentecostals. Now you mostly had to go to a baseball or football game to hear someone shout. But Evangelist Melvin still shouted. And shouted loud.

Zach felt something go through him every time the old man's voice got loud. In a rhythmic holler, something reverberated around Zach's empty soul like cannon fire in a western canyon.

Beads of sweat kept forming on Melvin Brankard's brow and on his upper lip. He would wipe them off with a pure white handkerchief.

But like the morning dew, the sweat would appear and reappear again. Then Evangelist Brankard would wipe them off. Again, and again, and again it happened.

His white shirt that looked like one ordered out of an old Sears and Roebuck catalog started to soak through. With his suit coat off, you could plainly watch the river of perspiration run. It started by his arms, then ran down the middle of his back, and then the front of his shirt was soaked too. But Evangelist Melvin was not the only one sweating. So was Zach.

A heavenly fire of conviction was drawing him. Something was gripping Zach that would not let him go. It was life changing and eternal. It was an answer to the prayers of the saints.

In his twenties, Zach had been a fiery orator. But then came the bigger offerings and the dumbing down of his message and delivery. Then came the corporate gatherings where Zach spoke for a fee. Along came TV contracts and media consultants who took everything away from Zach that offended. They also took away who he was and most of what helped set people free. He was religiously homogenized by people of the flesh.

Now Zach wore makeup and an invisible microphone by his ear and face. Zach was pro-everything and against nothing. Most of what he did was wood, hay, and stubble, awaiting the fire of the Judgment Seat of Christ (1 Corinthians 3:12). It was good but it wasn't preaching the Gospel of the Lord Jesus Christ. It wasn't eternal. It wasn't what Zach was called to do.

On the other hand, Evangelist Melvin

Brankard was pure gold. Gold tried by the fire. Everything that he did would stand up on God's Judgment Day. Bro. Melvin had never sold out. Bro. Melvin was like Naboth's vineyard in the Old Testament (1 Kings 21). Not for sale. The Gospel that Evangelist Melvin preached was a treasure buried in a lonely field. He had given all that he had for it.

Evangelist Melvin Brankard was a messenger from God to Zach Whitman that night. Bro. Melvin was that way to every church where he ministered. He always had been. And he always would be. That's what Bro. Melvin was called to do.

That's what Zach also had been called to do. But he hadn't been doing it. He had compromised. Evangelist Melvin hadn't compromised. He had been true to the heavenly Calling. Earth and Heaven needed more men and women like Melvin Brankard.

Every time Zach started to leave, another wisp of smoke of the prayers of the saints ascended into the holy place in Heaven. Sis. Vera Devon in Missouri, a teenager on the west coast, and Audubato Mufumbo in West Africa. Someday in Heaven they would find out how their prayers affected Zach Whitman. And their reward would be great.

Their prayers were so effective that, strangely, the message preached that night seemed like only a few minutes. Zach actually wished Bro. Melvin would preach longer; quite amazing coming from Zach, the communicator who flowed in sound bites of information. What a presence of God.

The last two and a half hours had almost felt

to Zach like he had been in a fog. The fog was about to lift. It was then that Zach began to realize that Evangelist Melvin was standing on the hardwood aisle at the end of Zach's row.

"Young brother, come here! I want to lay my hands on you!" said Bro. Melvin to Zach.

Like an automated robot, Zach stood up and started to sob and weep almost uncontrollably. Zach was glad that he hadn't brought his crusade security bodyguards with him. They would have pushed Bro. Melvin away. Just like Zach had been pushing Jesus away.

"Young brother, look into my eyes. *Thou art the chosen of the Lord, called to do thy Master's bidding. But the enemy hath desired to sift thee as wheat,"* said Bro. Melvin. "I see you in a room with high ceilings. Long silk drapes by some kind of French doors. And a computer on a stylish desk."

"My God, he is describing my room at the Four Seasons," Zach thought.

Bro. Melvin—or rather, God's *Spirit* in Bro. Melvin—wasn't done yet: "And you are crying within and saying, 'God, if you can hear me, speak to me.' Even now, the *Lord thy God* speaks to thee. Thou hast left thy first love. Thy lamp is almost out. But the Lord shall refine thee. The Lord shall equip thee. The Lord shall *restore* thee. The Lord shall break through thy pride. He shall take thee to the Potter's House to be shaped into another vessel. A vessel of *honor*, ready for the Master's use."

The God that Evangelist Melvin Brankard served spoke in King James English, and his God spoke loudly.

"Young man, raise your hands," said Bro.

Melvin to Zach.

Limp as a rag, Zach stood crying. Actually, sobbing would be a better term.

Unknown on Earth yet celebrated in Heaven, Bro. Melvin continued to *flow* in the Gifts of the Spirit mentioned in the New Testament (1 Corinthians 12). Something was moving and stirring in that service that helped change the world. No one saw them. Nobody knew they were there, but angels actually were lined up against the wall watching the old man minister.

Every once in a while, one of the "robed in white" would say, "I'm going over to stand by him. I sense the presence of the one we love on him." Often, they would linger until the last person quit praying or until the old man left the building.

With great interest and love for Zach, they watched. One angel said to another, "I've never desired to go to that man Zach's meetings. And the Lord has never sent me. But I sense something drawing me toward him tonight."

Another angel said, "Tonight God sent me here to help him." Then, invisible to human sight, the angelic wonder that stood about nine feet tall glided with two of his friends over to Zach and Bro. Melvin's side. They were ministering spirits sent from the Lord.

Zach, who was known all over the Earth, gave Gospel speeches all alone night after night. No one from Heaven stood or sat with him in the recording studio day after day. When you have no representation from Heaven in your meetings, you really are alone, even though thousands of people are in attendance.

Zach was shaking and had trembling lips, and the anointing of God was starting to melt his hard heart. Right about then, Evangelist Melvin Brankard took his strong right hand and laid it right on Zach's one hundred and twenty-five-dollar haircut.

As the old evangelist reached out, so did the kind angel. An unseen hand. Another smiling angel reached right through Zach's designer coat. That heavenly hand reached right through twenty years of pain, and in one touch broke down every religious wall Zach had ever built. Talk about "somebody touched me."

9

The Man in the Purple Trousers

Zach's red, puffy eyes opened a little bit as he lay on the floor. The smell of olive oil was on his hair. It was also on the back of his leather coat. And peace was in his heart.

The first thing Zach saw at a side angle was a pair of black industrial shoes and white socks. His eyes followed up the purple trousers, past the silver tie bar, and into the eyes of God's love. The old usher had been sitting there all alone in the church beside Bro. Zach for hours.

Even though he had to get up at 5:30 in the morning, he stayed. Not only stayed, but he stayed and prayed. The old man's ministry was to lock up the house of God after service. It had been his ministry for over thirty years. The pastor could always depend on him. Every light was shut off. The air conditioning or heat dial was set just right. Not very impressive to man but extremely impressive to Jesus.

Everyone in Glory knew the man. The robed in white talked about him. They looked forward to him coming to Heaven. *In the land where the first are last and the last are first, the old usher was famous.* What a glorious entrance into the Celestial City would be his. He would shine with the glory of God forever like the stars in the firmament. The man had done what he could. Used what he had. Been found faithful. And Heaven knew all about it.

The usher in the purple suit wrapped his arms around Zach and helped pull him to his feet. They were arms that were still strong from many years of manual labor. Arms that held a worldwide ministry as he helped Bro. Zach get up off the floor.

"That was a mighty powerful blessing you got tonight, Brother," said the usher.

"Where has everyone gone?" asked Zach.

"Oh, they've all gone home."

It seemed to Zach that he had been on the floor for a few minutes, but it had really been for about three hours. A few times, the driver of the car service Zach used had come in to check on him. When Zach had stepped out of the car a few hours earlier, he had ordered the driver, "Whatever you do, don't leave me here. Stay until I come out!"

The last time the driver checked on him, he was muttering on his way out, "I better get paid for this! And what kind of a nut house is this church!" Well, the man would get paid. Zach's American Express card account would take care of that. And yes, in the eyes of the world, this church was a nut house. But in Heaven and on Earth, it was holy ground.

"Oh, I almost forgot to give you this," said the usher in the purple suit.

Zach opened the piece of folded paper ripped out of a 99-cent tablet. It said:

Room 112 at the Midtown Motel. I want to see you.

- M. L. Brankard.

No gold embossed stationery like Zach used at his ministry. A priceless message on cheap paper. A message sent from Heaven.

The old usher had to steady Zach as he walked up the slight incline toward the back of the church. Zach was somewhere between quite unsteady and drunk. Drunk on the new wine from Jesus.

A different Zach walked out than the Zach that had strutted into Temple of the Living God. That is the way church is supposed to be. It is the way your church can be. That's what an encounter with the Lord Jesus Christ does. One service changed his whole life forever. Zach would never ever be the same.

The old usher smiled with the love of Jesus. He also kept saying over and over again, "Praise the Lord. Praise the Lord," as he helped Zach into the back seat of a black Lincoln Continental Executive Series town car.

Zach never saw the old usher again but he never forgot him. His kindness always stayed with Zach. Half a lifetime later, the old man waited for Zach on a distant shore. When Zach crossed the river, how they embraced. No more purple suits. The next time they met they would both be robed in white.

But in the here and now, a slightly mumbling driver closed the Lincoln car door and off into the night Zach went. After Zach handed the driver a tip of two one-hundred-dollar bills, peace came onto the Lincoln car driver. They were two one-hundred-dollar bills that should have gone into the offering plate.

"Run everything else on this American Express card," Zach told the driver. And off to the Midtown Motel they went. Off toward Zach's destiny

10

The Healing Booth

The shiny black Lincoln pulled right in front of the Midtown Motel. It had been a long time since such a car had driven into that yard. Only poor people and mostly truckers sleeping in their cabs went there.

Zach thought to himself, "What a dump this motel is." Even though Zach had received a

touch from God, his mind wasn't totally renewed. That would come.

Zach's spirit within kept leading him to
search for the old preacher man who had prayed
for him. The tug on Zach within kept him searching until he found the room where the man of
God stayed. There was a note on the door that
said:

Bro. Zach, meet me across the street at
the Triangle Diner.

Again, no fancy stationery. Just a Post-It
note. Zach had secretaries that wrote to people
messages that really meant very little on gold
embossed stationery. But Zach had received a
message that would further change his whole

world, and it was on a very humble piece of paper. Humble pieces of paper and humble people can do a lot for God.

Looking down the old Main Street, Zach saw the neon sign. The diner looked like a 1950s holdover. Like something out of an old Alfred Hitchcock movie. But inside at the last booth sat hope. Inside was help. Inside, at the last booth on the right sat Melvin Brankard.

Zach walked past the fancy but mostly tasteless pastries, beyond the cash register counter with mints and newspapers, right past empty booth after empty booth. And there he was. A man sent from God.

The white-haired, old patriarch was back to and not even facing him. The old evangelist was sitting silently, eating a late-night lunch of toast and grape jelly.

Zach extended his hand, and on autopilot started his stage-crafted greeting. But before he could start, the old preacher spoke first.

"Hello, son," he said in a voice edged by years of revival. Just warm, loving words, truly spoken from a pure heart of gold.

Zach sat down and couldn't even speak. Now, that in and of itself was a miracle. Then Zach took one look into Melvin Brankard's eyes and just started to cry. A pure release of tears. Not convulsing tears. Not sobbing tears. Just a steady rain on Zach's barren, thirsty soul. The dry parched desert within was being watered by God's love. Amazingly, Zach couldn't say much, but he was willing to listen. And again, that in itself was a very strange thing.

Zach Whitman always—and I mean always—had something to say. And Zach

Whitman never listened. He liked to hear himself talk. But in a little diner, a very strange alignment of the preacher planets took place. The preacher with everything had nothing. And the preacher with nothing had everything. And Zach sat in silence.

It's amazing how a broken spirit and a contrite heart can tie up an orator's tongue. It can also open up their heart. That's exactly what happened to Zach.

After Zach sat there for about five minutes, there was a hand that reached across the table and rested on Zach's gym-exercised arm. That hand reached across the years and pulled Zach Whitman out of the miry clay. The hand of Evangelist Melvin Brankard had another hand on it. The hand of Jesus. A nail-scarred hand that reached right through every hurt. A hand that smoothed out every valley in Zach's life. *The Potter's hand.*

In about five minutes, that hand supernaturally smoothed out the rough edges in Zach's personality. The cockiness departed. The self-will and arrogance evaporated. In that corner booth on the end, a holy, heavenly mist of real, heartfelt humility came down.

"I think I'm done preaching," Zach said. "I'm a hypocrite. I don't even know who I am. I'm sure not who I've tried so hard to be. I'm sure not who people think that I am. I've lost my way... I've lost my way," Zach kept repeating over and over again, as he just sat there and cried some more.

And then here came *the voice*. It was kind of a roughhewn and chiseled voice. A voice like a director wants to have narrating on a national public broadcasting program. It was a voice that had another voice in it. The voice of truth. The voice of love. The voice of Jesus wrapped up in the voice of Melvin Brankard:

"Son, you are just getting started," the old evangelist said. "You might tarry a while until the right side of your beard grows back"—this referring to the Old Testament story of King David's ambassadors (2 Samuel 10).

Zach knew the story, though he had never thought of it or heard anyone speak about it in over twenty years. Yet strangely, Zach knew what Bro. Melvin meant.

Like a boy in a Sunday School class, Zach listened and asked questions. And often, he pulled another napkin out of the silver holder to dry his watery eyes.

"What about my ministry? It is all built on

me," said Zach. "What about my marriage? Tara doesn't love me anymore."

"Son, Jesus can fix anything. Keep a *pure* relationship with the Lord Jesus Christ, and every other relationship that you have will be okay."

Evangelist Melvin reached for a napkin himself in the old silver napkin holder. Bro. Melvin wasn't crying but he needed something to write on. In large, plain letters, he printed "MESSAGE," then slid the napkin toward Zach. He had also written "PREACH JESUS AND NOT YOURSELF."

Then the old evangelist said, "Lift Jesus up. Preach about Heaven, where we will be with Jesus. Preach about the soon coming of the Savior. And stay humble. God can replace you *just like that*," the words were quickly spoken while Evangelist Melvin snapped two seventy-five-year-old fingers together. Then, looking right through him with eyes of love and steel, Evangelist Melvin said this:

"If I was still a pastor, I wouldn't even let you preach for me. I know the whole world might like you, but the Holy Ghost might not be that impressed with you. If HE was impressed, then HE would show up in your meetings! Why aren't people saved in your meetings? Why aren't they healed?"

Then in a low, gravelly voice, a voice with no condemnation but filled with truth, came these words: *"You are just running a spa for the saved.* It's entertainment. It's fluff. And it won't keep people out of hell. It won't set the captive free. We are all going to stand before God someday. *What are you going to say about the opportunity God gave you?*

"Son, you would never make it on the *sawdust trail* where I came from," Bro. Melvin said referring to the old campmeetings where they would pour sawdust out on the floor. "If you will start preaching under the anointing instead of giving feel-good speeches, God is going to show up in your life in a *big* way! God's not mad at you either."

Grace met Zach at a little diner in the middle of the night. At 2:45 a.m., Zach fell in love with Jesus and the foolishness of preaching again. He fell in love with what he used to love. Revival came pouring into his soul. And Zach felt more alive than he ever had.

Now it was time to leave and certain sadness came upon Zach. In old-time Judea, people sensed it as Jesus left. Zach sensed it now. He just really hated to see the old man go.

"Bro. Brankard, where do you go next?"

"I go to Borger, Texas."

"OK," said Zach. "Then where?"

"And then I go to North Little Rock, Arkansas."

"How can I reach you?"

"My sister, Edith, lives in Abilene, Texas and always knows the number where I'm at." Bro. Brankard had divine connections but didn't ever use the cellphone he kept packed in his suitcase.

Zach started to walk away, but then with tears streaming down his face, he abruptly turned and embraced the old man.

It was then that the old patriarch of the Gospel put both of his seasoned hands on Zach's shoulders. Evangelist Melvin looked him right in the eyes, and like an Old Testament prophet, he started to speak. In a low and holy, yet richly modulated voice, words from Heaven came:

"The Word of the Lord is this: Go before my people and repent. Repent wholeheartedly. Separate yourself from unbelieving believers who have attached themselves to you. The mixed multitude of which you have been a part shall not go into the Promised Land. Step aside for a season. A season of prayer. A season of listening. A season of much. Even much peace. Return to your first love. You are a chosen vessel. Many are called but few are chosen. And take up your cross and follow me." Then Evangelist Melvin started saying multiple hallelujahs and "Amen, brother."

A late-night waitress had boot polish black

colored hair, with a white strip down the side, and looked like she had seen a ghost. She had. The Holy Ghost in operation.

It was then that Evangelist Melvin turned to her and said, "Do not have that abortion. For the life within thee is precious. And the prayers of thy mother are going to be answered. Even now, they ascend continually before the throne room of God, both day and night."

"How on earth did you know that?" the waitress said as she burst into tears of repentance. "Do you know my mother? Has she been talking to you?"

"Cool," said a biker nearby as he scurried away before the Holy Ghost radar got on his backslidden life."

So, it was 3:00 a.m. and Zach had collapsed on his face in a diner booth—head on the table by the Heinz ketchup bottle, with arms stretched straight out, crying. Really crying. Loudly crying. In fact, sobbing would be more like it. And a waitress was sitting on a counter stool with her head in both her hands, saying, "Jesus, forgive me. Oh, Jesus, please forgive me. I was going to kill my baby."

"He will, little sister. He really will. He already has," said Evangelist Melvin to the waitress.

About this time, a customer came in for coffee and abruptly decided that he didn't need a cup of coffee. The customer sure left a mighty lot quicker than he had come in.

The cook came out of the kitchen and said, "What the (blank) is going on here?" as he took a look at the crying waitress and convulsing, sobbing Zach. But it was the eyes on Melvin

Brankard that scared the living daylights out of him. Eyes that looked like Charlton Heston playing Moses in *The Ten Commandments* movie.

Those eyes would have scared the devil out of the cook, but he ran outside saying, "I have to have a cigarette, and I have to have it *now!*" pushing the swinging doors so hard that they sounded like they would come right off their hinges. They just kept swinging and swinging back and forth on those same hinges like they were electrically powered.

Zach couldn't sit up but he was listening to everything going on. With his head on the table by the ketchup bottle and salt and pepper, he prayed in tongues. He then said within himself, "I'd give all that I own to be used like that for five minutes and be a mouthpiece for God."

It was right then that the old Evangelist

turned quickly and walked right over to the booth where Zach sat sprawled out on the table. The old man pulled him to his feet, saying,

"I LAY MY HANDS UPON YOU WITH THE APOSTOLIC ANOINTING GIVEN TO ME BY THE LORD JESUS CHRIST. And you shall flow. The flow of My Spirit from this night shall never leave thee. It shall flow unto the nations. A mighty river shall rise up within you. The waters shall quench thee within. You shall be a mighty sword of the spirit in My hand to usher in the second coming of the Lord. I will make thy name great in Heaven and on the Earth."

Zach didn't pass out but he came real close—in the middle of the night and in the middle of the Triangle Diner.

Impartation happened to Zach that very night through the prophetic laying on of hands.

What Zach didn't believe in happened to him.

Most churches don't believe in it. But Jesus does. So did the Apostle Paul. So does the *New Testament*. The *Spirit* makes all the difference.

Zach became quite a believer in the laying on of hands that very night. A man with an experience is never at the mercy of a man with an argument. Just because a lot of churches and preachers don't do something doesn't mean that God doesn't want it done. But when God wants to do something, he has to find a vessel.

God found one that night named Zach at the Triangle Diner. God already had a vessel named Melvin Brankard. The great thing about God is that one of his full vessels can be poured into an empty vessel. In fact, just one of God's full vessels can be poured out to change the world. The gift of God came in. Zach Whitman never

ever was the same.

The young man started to fall out on the diner floor, but the old evangelist caught Zach by the lapels on his eight-hundred-dollar coat. He put one arm around Zach, one of Zach's arms around his neck, and sort of carried Zach out of the diner. He carried him out of bondage.

Jesus in the old man saved Zach's ministry and saved Zach's marriage. Jesus in Melvin Brankard totally changed the future of Zach's children. Even one that wasn't yet born. A child not even conceived but Heaven knew was destined to come. That's what Jesus can do. In the middle of the night in a tiny diner, right after a Holy Ghost meeting in a little white clapboard-siding church that's on the wrong side of the tracks.

So, arm in arm, they approached the black

Lincoln Continental Executive Series town car. The sleepy, frustrated driver was nodding off when he opened his eyes to see Zach being carried towards him.

"What the (blank) did you have to drink in there?" the astonished driver said.

The car service driver had driven for lots of drunks. But he had never driven for a drunk talking in tongues. A drunk talking in tongues and being carried by another drunk talking in tongues, all the while going back and forth between "THANK YOU, JESUS" and tongues.

The tongues were starting to get to the driver. But then he felt a presence. It was just too much for the cussin' Lincoln driver. With a scared and freaked out look in his eyes, the driver screamed, "I quit!" and drove off, leaving two evangelists standing in the dust. This evening, driving someone to church and picking them up after church had been too wild a night for him.

The sound of squealing tires and tongue talking filled the air. There was the smell of exhaust and anointing oil. And then Zach did something that he hadn't done in a long time.

He laughed.

More than a chuckle. Not a dignified, smiling laugh. But a howling, high-pitched, roll-on-the-side-of-the-curb cackle. Not very polite. Just uproarious, gleeful, hold your sides, donkey-like "hee-haw" sounds. And then the old evangelist joined in and laughed too. Laughed till he cried.

He sat down on the curb beside Zach while tipping his head back heavenward. They made a sound any comedian would die to hear from an audience. It came in waves. Zach would nearly settle down and Bro. Melvin would ignite.

The Texas wind carried a joyful sound that night. Two preachers. Two evangelists sitting on a curb in the dust, completely saturated in joy. A joy that religion and the world can't give. A joy that can never be taken away.

11

Room 112 at the Midtown

The old Evangelist laughed at Zach so hard
that the two bottom buttons on the
Hawaiian shirt that he wore every night after
church came unbuttoned. Zach's cell phone was
lost and he didn't even care. Imagine that. Talk
about a night of miracles.

The old man stood up from the curb and

spontaneously messed up Zach's hair. "Son, you're a mess," said Bro. Melvin. Zach's hair stood straight up like a rooster's tail. Put enough olive oil on anyone's hair in a prayer line and they have a new hairstyle. That was certainly the case with smiling and laughing Evangelist Zach.

"Well, son, Jesus doesn't leave anyone in the ditch, so I'm going to invite you into the palace," referring to the Midtown Motel. "I also want to show you a new invention. It's called a landline phone," said a snickering Bro. Melvin. And then they started laughing again.

In his early years, Zach had quite a sense of humor. Religion and being lukewarm had killed it. Tonight, his sense of humor came back home. It was the first time in about a decade that Zach had really laughed. Hard to imagine that, but it was true. And for the first time in a mighty long time, Evangelist Zach had made a friend. A forever friend. A God-sent friend.

The metal key with a green plastic number 112 attached to it opened the room and the two men of God stepped inside. Evangelist Melvin moved some things off one of the beds so that Bro. Zach would have a place to sit.

On the floor he placed a Thompson Chain Reference Bible. Then a Strong's Concordance big enough to knock out an intruder; a Vine's word study book, and a pack of Canadian peppermints, all willingly moved so Zach could have his own bed.

What a bed it was. This bed had a fake leather headboard made out of vinyl. An aluminum heat radiator with a dented top was on the left side of the room. It had a red button that you'd push for heat and a round dial to turn up the fan. The room was a refugee from the early 1970s.

Its light brown paneling was bulged out a little bit in certain places on the wall, and it had a drop ceiling with fluorescent lights that sort of gradually came on.

There was an orange Formica counter by the sink with cigarette burns on it from long ago. And inside the sink was a small rust stain around the drain.

The shower in the bathroom looked like an old upright phone booth with three sides sprayed in a white enamel coating—a coating that was starting to chip in places. Yet, into that holy place Zach Whitman came.

He opened up, and talked, and cried, and prayed with the old evangelist for hours. Unaware that the course of his life and ministry were being set on a trajectory of blessing like nothing he had ever seen before. Grace takes you where you don't deserve to go. And God's grace keeps you there.

Bro. Melvin told Zach of God's grace and mercy in his own life and ministry and of God's keeping power. The old man said, "Zach, God has kept me through the years," and he told the young man of chances he had years ago to be bitter and to give up. Times when doors shut, but then something *so much better opened wide.* Those small disappointments had really been God's appointments.

Bro. Melvin shared how God had taught him to keep the ministry debt free. He also shared how he could have neglected his family but didn't. "Zach, I've pleased the Lord. I've done my assignment."

The old man began to hum softly. Then he started to sing in a half lullaby and half hymn sort of way. The old song just sort of flowed through him. And angels stood and listened by thin drapes with a drawstring that didn't quite close in the middle.

He sang softly, "It's not the first mile that's so important, It's the last mile when day is done, Then you'll see Jesus in all His splendor, And He will have for you the crown you've won."

In little motel room 112, the sanctifying power came on Zach Whitman. And it came to stay.

As the morning light broke, Zach said, "I've lost my phone."

Bro. Melvin laughingly said, "There's that new invention," and pointed toward the corner of the room.

Zach then used a landline phone for the first time in years. One phone call to his administrative assistant and he was back in the loop, soon to be picked up. He then told Bro. Melvin, "I'm supposed to be on national TV in a couple days, but I think I'm going to cancel."

But Bro. Melvin replied, "I have some kind of a check in my spirit when you talk about canceling."

That was the world that Evangelist Melvin Brankard lived in. A world of Holy Ghost checks and balances. A simple world of peace or the momentary lack of it.

For Bro. Melvin, what the Word said was number one. Then him having peace in his spirit was next. He obeyed the Word and always followed the peace of God. Bro. Zach got a glimpse into that world that night.

"I sense that you ought to not cancel but go on and tell what great things that the Lord has done," said Bro. Melvin.

And so it was. The peace of God settled into room 112 at the Midtown. And Zach followed that peace.

The young evangelist stayed in beautiful hotels all around the world. He would walk out of those luxurious rooms and never feel a twinge about leaving. Never look back. Never really care if he ever saw the place again. But Zach really hated to leave this humble little place. Room 112 with the outdated orange counter by the sink.

"I need to go home," Zach said. "Can you come with me? Because I don't ever want to lose the peace that I sense when I'm around you."

"No, I have work to do here. Call me when

things get settled. Everything is going to be alright, Bro. Zach. And I will be praying for you."

The next twenty years, they would talk on the phone every week, sometimes several times a week. Often, they would spend days at a time together. Bro. Melvin's days of staying in cheap motels were about to be over. Zach's days of running from God were all gone.

Everything God had ever taught Bro. Melvin, Bro. Melvin would teach Bro. Zach. Everything the Spirit had imparted to Bro. Melvin, God used to impart to Bro. Zach. It was the New Testament way. It was what the Apostle Paul did with Timothy. It was what Paul meant when he said in Scripture, "For though you might have ten thousand instructors in Christ, yet you do not have many fathers." (1

Corinthians 4:15 NKJV).

Zach Whitman, like most preachers, was a ministerial orphan. He had never had a father in the Lord. But Zach sure had one now. And when the car picked him up and Zach rode away, he was turned around in the backseat waving like a little kid. Waving goodbye to the old evangelist in a bright Hawaiian shirt standing outside. The saint on the sidewalk in front of the Midtown Motel. The man God used to forever change his life.

12

Prayer That Prevails

The ministry jet pointed heavenward and Zach was headed home. As he arrived, the radiant rays of sunshine were bathing Zach's beautiful home in light. The house had always been beautiful on the outside. Now it would be beautiful on the inside too.

Zach had always been all about the outside

of life. How things appeared and looked on the outside. The only part of life that most people see. After spending time with Bro. Melvin, he would forever be about the inside, where the heart is. The part of a person that God looks at. Bro. Melvin had taught him that when the inside is right, the outside just kind of takes care of itself.

Zach walked through the front door and his steps felt light. There was peace in his heart. Zach was the right man to drive the oppressive spirit out of his own home that had lingered there for years.

Zach deserved a divorce. He deserved alimony and separation. But thank God we don't have to get what we deserve. Instead, mercy found him. And mercy's best friend, God's grace, found him too. Those two are always together.

Mercy and grace had Zach's wife, Tara, see him as he approached the front entrance. There she was, at the top of the grand staircase in the main foyer, like an old black and white Turner Classic Movie. Grace and mercy were the directors.

Tara started to cry when she saw him. She walked down the staircase even as Zach started coming through the front door. At first, Tara cried thinking Zach was on drugs. His eyes were so different. His whole demeanor had changed.

That's what happens when you no longer are oppressed by the enemy. You can get a forever touch from God in a moment's times. Anyone can. A life-changing moment that lasts for eternity.

Over and over, Zach kept sobbing and

saying, "Forgive me. Please forgive me. Can you ever forgive me?" And tears of joy came to Tara that maybe her husband really did love God and also still loved her too.

Human forgiveness has its limits. God's mercy has none. Something came on Tara, and it was supernatural and divine. It was a generational moment and it would affect every one of their descendants. A seed of forgiveness is a forever seed.

They embraced and while they held each other, someone else's strong arms wrapped around them. Hope came and embraced Zach and Tara. And hope would never ever let them go.

Then hope's best friend came and embraced Tara. Hope's best friend named *faith*. They are never far apart. They just really like each other.

The two are inseparable. If you ever meet the one, you will have the chance to meet the other.

When hope and faith were done with Zach and Tara, they would also be inseparable. Again, if you ever meet hope, you will have the chance to meet faith also, and together they will bring Heaven into your life.

That's what happened to Tara at the bottom of a beautiful, winding staircase. Something supernatural took place. It was a wonder. You wonder how it happened. That's what God does. It was totally unexplainable.

Into that embrace of Zach, Tara, hope, and faith, came also the *greatest of all*: Love came in. Love wrapped its eternal arms around the other four and just kind of squeezed them all together. A three-minute, life-changing yet eternal embrace. Or I guess that you could call it a hug from Heaven. Whatever it was called, it worked. The five of them would never be parted from that moment on. Tara and Zach, hope, faith, and love.

Yes, something certainly was different about Zach's eyes. They reminded Tara of someone she used to know. The Zach she fell in love with and married. The Zach who made her laugh. He now had eyes that Jesus could look through. And it sure made everything look different. Zach was back. Tara's very best friend and soulmate who had been gone for so long.

For so many years, the ministry had been everything and his wife nothing. Like a politician's wife, Tara had played the game and stood on stage. Tara's plastic smile was always part of the show. Two plastic and broken people that Jesus loved. Their strength and self-effort were all gone when Jesus came. And that was a good thing. For when I am weak, I am *strong* (2 Corinthians 12:10).

"Tara, I've been so horrible to live with. So selfish," Zach said. "I've been blinded by ambition. So driven. Somewhere I stopped being the husband and father I should be. I stopped loving God and loving people. I've been miserable. I've made everyone around me miserable too. Can you ever forgive me?"

Zach continued, "My most important ministry is you. It is always going to be from now on. I'm going to take at least three months off. I'm not going to preach again until the Lord and you think that I'm ready. I'm not going to preach until I have my house in order. It's my fault. All of it is my entire fault."

Simply put: The Holy Ghost in five minutes

did what five years of negotiations and coun-
seling could never do.

While Zach and Tara had been embracing on the
stairs, a lot of things had been happening in the
spirit. In the early morning Nebraska light, a
farmer sensed a deep stirring to pray. He did.
Walking outside the barn, the unknown farmer
dropped everything and let the chores wait. He
interceded. The farmer interceded for Zach and
Tara, though he never knew them and never
would in this life.

In the middle of the day in London,
England, a great Nigerian pastor was visiting the
European continent. While in his hotel room, the
pastor broke forth in a glorious tongue. It was

glorious alright. More glorious than tongue could ever tell. Heaven heard and answered.

Those prayers covered a precious couple named Zach and Tara at the bottom of the stairs. Those prayers also birthed Zach's destiny. A destiny planned by God from the very foundation of the Earth.

It could not come to pass until Zach repented and got right with God. But the very moment that Zach repented, the Holy Spirit started putting glorious things in motion for Zach and Tara that had always been in the mind of God. God doesn't hold grudges. Neither did an angel of a woman named Tara.

The Nigerian pastor and Nebraskan farmer's prayers lit the fuse on the glory to come. Waves of glory that Zach would be prominent in bringing to Earth. The pastor and farmer's prayers changed the world. They would never know until they got to Heaven. But God knew.

One of those waves of glory supernaturally hit in Ohio. This floodtide would soon cover the Ohio River Valley and flow all over the Midwest and into lower Canada. Here's what had happened in the twinkling of an eye:

Something jumped in the spirit from Nebraska and London to a staff meeting at a megachurch in Ohio. There is no time or distance in prayer. In the staff meeting, the pastor of the megachurch started to cry and said, "I feel like standing up and worshipping and praying in the Spirit." He then said, "That is probably only me," and started to sip his Starbucks coffee and read a report, when he suddenly stood up and obeyed the Lord.

Heaven came down. The boring weekly

scheduled routine suddenly turned into a camp-meeting. All of a sudden, people were literally lying on the floor. They were interceding with joy unspeakable. From out back of a barn in Nebraska, and from a London hotel room, the power of God had landed. All because somebody obeyed and prayed.

When the farmer went back to his chores, he sensed an incredible peace. That's how it works in prayer. He knew that the victory had come. The Nigerian pastor in his hotel room went back to a book he was writing with great peace and joy. If only they could have seen and known what they had done—what the Spirit had done through them. Someday they would. Someday robed in white.

The lukewarm church staff had been strate-gically planning, but the Holy Spirit had an agenda and plan also. When the fire hit, the lukewarmness left. The intercessory spirit in that staff then prayed for Jesus to heal Zach and Tara's home, though they did not know it.

They also prayed for God to send Zach their way, though they knew not what they prayed in tongues with groanings that could not be uttered. Their prayers were heard. They always are.

In a short two years, Zach would hold a 10-week revival at that megachurch. The pastor and staff didn't know it would happen. Zach didn't know it would happen. But the Spirit knew. Heaven placed it on the schedule that day—the day people at the staff meeting got slain out in the spirit. They had interceded in the heavenly language, praying in other tongues as the Holy Spirit gave the utterance and prayed through them.

Melvin Brankard would teach the morning Bible studies at the 10-week revival in Ohio to large, growing crowds. At night, people would line up hours before service just to get a seat. It would be a real, Heaven-sent, prayed-down revival.

Salvations, healings, and scores of men and women would be called into the ministry. Churches would be started that would change the culture of cities. A mighty move of God that would change a whole region of the nation was put on the calendar that day. The outcome of an American presidential election would also be changed by God's glorious grace because people prayed. Prayed in faith. And it all started in a conference room in Ohio that day. Signs and wonders began in the spirit right there.

That precious pastor in Ohio and his lovely wife would be kept from scandal and divorce. After Zach preached that revival, a 7,000-seat auditorium would need to be built, and still they would need two Sunday morning services. Missionaries would come from that church. And Zach Whitman would become a spiritual father in the Lord to that pastor.

No, that wasn't on the agenda of the staff meeting. But that's what they got. In fact, the pastor was bored when he went. But then the Holy Spirit was invited in. The Spirit knocked and they answered. That's what they got when the pastor yielded to the Spirit.

The pastor almost missed it. But he didn't. The more he yielded, the more the pastor loosened up. Half spinning and half dancing, he spilled his Starbucks coffee on his sweater and his dead demographics sheet. And he prayed with exceedingly great joy.

Prayer makes hard things easy. That's why things would seem so easy for Zach and Tara. It was the prayers of the saints. Prayers prayed by people unknown on Earth yet well known in Heaven. Connected in the spirit and someday to each other. All because of answered prayer, the impossible became possible. Their prayers brought rays of divine comfort on the Earth.

All this happened while Zach and Tara, hope, faith, and love embraced at the bottom of a staircase. Because Zach was right with God, his destiny could begin to be birthed. Ministering spirits called angels came into a wealthy suburb in Texas and healed Zach and Tara Whitman's home. Like shafts of light going up, the prayers ascended. And from the throne of God, the presence of God descended to minister and to heal. After this, Zach and Tara went out to breakfast and talked and talked—and talked some more.

All this happened while Evangelist Melvin Brankard slept like a baby. He always did. And the angels that traveled with him stood nearby— by the heat radiator with a dent on the top, right by the curtains with a drawstring that never quite closes all the way in the middle.

13

The Zach with New Eyes

The following day, Zach and Tara stepped out of the limo at the Christian TV network, and for the first time in a long time, they stepped out hand in hand. There was nothing wrong with the Christian TV network. It was a mighty tool in the end-time proclamation of the Gospel. There had been something wrong with Zach. Zach had been the problem. Jesus in Zach was the solution.

As they stepped out of the backseat of the car, cameras flashed. Excited tourists and partners who were there for the evening taping pointed. They proclaimed in loud voices, *"There he is!" "Oh, look! It's Zach Whitman!"*

Hands were outstretched and autographs sought for. It had almost a mini Academy Awards feel. It wasn't what Christ died for, but a lot of ministers would sure be willing to do whatever it took to be there. It was the kind of acclaim that a lot of ministers and Christians craved. Mostly good people who mostly had good hearts.

Zach knew the drill. He had been there a hundred times. But the Zach arriving tonight had a new heart.

Walking down the hall, Zach suddenly

found himself looking at people differently. It was amazing. It was like the lights had come on in Zach's spirit. The blind now could see. He now could see what others were blind to and either couldn't or didn't want to see. When you can see the Lord in people, they look pretty good. When you can't see the Lord in them, they look mighty empty, regardless of how fancy or rich they are.

On the way in, Zach saw a humble little laborer who had worked there for years. He did behind the scenes work of moving cables and such and mostly manual labor. A glorified fetch-it man for the skilled engineer crowd. Zach instantly knew him in the spirit.

He sensed what a good man he was. What a pure heart he had. How this mostly forgotten and noticed by nobody man was praying that people would get saved and find Jesus through tonight's telecast. That humble man stood out to Zach just like the man stood out to God.

Right then, Zach was a lot more impressed by that man behind the camera than he was with himself. Years ago, Zach wouldn't have given him the time of day. He would have thought of the man as a lowlife. Now, Zach wished that the man was his friend.

In years to come, the man would become one of Zach's best friends. Zach would hire him and triple his salary. Countless times Zach had the man come to his home and blessed him. Zach put all of the man's children through Bible school. And one of them ended up administrating much of Zach's worldwide ministry.

Zach didn't know all that would happen when he walked by. But Zach did discern this:

He knew how great the man's reward would be on Judgment Day. And Zach sensed a deep longing within the worker's heart to please the Lord.

The day is coming when we will all stand before God. The Word of God plainly states that all of us have that appointment to be judged. There will be no exceptions. There will be no excuses. Either you have accepted Jesus as your Savior or you haven't. Either you go to Heaven or to hell. Grace had saved Zach from hell and from himself. Jesus will do the same for anyone. All that you have to do is ask in faith.

Judgment Day is when we will all give an account of what we did with what we had to work with. We will give an account of not just what we did, but why we did it.

Zach had been given a lot and done very

little. The fetch-it man had been given little but had done a lot with it. He had done his best for God's glory. Zach had done his best for Zach's glory. But that was all about to change for Zach. Zach knew and Heaven knew.

With his new prophetic eyes, Zach mostly just saw the good in people. It was like some kind of Holy Ghost radar had been turned on in his spirit. That's exactly what it was. A radar that wouldn't shut off. A radar that Zach didn't want to ever shut off.

In years to come, his spiritual father would teach him more of how to yield to it and how to be a blessing by flowing in the anointed Gifts of the Spirit.

A part of Zach was so alive. Another part of him had died, never to live again. Yes, the old Zach was dead and buried and gone. The new

Zach had extra sensory perception from another world. Zach had been with Jesus and Zach had been with Evangelist Melvin Brankard. Jesus and Bro. Brankard spent all day together every day. And they both loved each other. And they both loved Bro. Zach.

There were no stones to throw in Zach's revived hands. No condemnation in his heart. Only a fresh fountain of God's love that had been opened up deep within his spirit. Tonight, it would flow. It would flow from deep within to the thirsty, barren desert in America and around the world. Like the woman at the well who met Jesus, Zach had found everything he had always been thirsty for. He had living water to drink. He had living water to share. And Zach would never thirst again.

About that same time, Zach saw a haughty

set director with a clipboard barking out orders. Inside, Zach just knew that the man didn't care for the Gospel of Jesus Christ. For the set director, it was a job. A filler until he could get something better. Other people raced around doing the same. Some were faithful believers. Others were not. They were just there to build their resume, then off to something perceived as more impressive they would go. Not called; they were opportunistic.

Zach knew. For most of his life, he had been the same way. "For sale" to the highest bidder. What used to be so impressive to Zach wasn't quite that way anymore. People that used to really ring Zach's bell did nothing for him now. Pride had always made Zach label people. What they had done and what they could do for Zach was what counted. Zach felt differently now.

People that Zach used to feel were beneath him were now brothers and sisters of the King of Kings. Everybody is somebody to Jesus, and Zach knew it. He loved everybody and stopped judging people. No more condescending looks. Zach knew how often he had missed it. He knew how deceived he himself had always been in so many areas. If God did show Zach something wrong about someone's life, he just prayed for them and sensed a certain sadness.

That's what Jesus would have done if He walked the Earth, if He were walking into a network to be on TV. Yet, Jesus did still walk the Earth. Jesus was going on TV tonight: Jesus in Zach.

High above the lights in the studio, the angels gathered. They wanted to hear what Zach had to say. They sensed the Spirit of Jesus whom they worship on Zach.

Somewhere out by a streetlight, two heavenly, angelic creatures parted ways. One was going to Evangelist Melvin's meeting and could hardly wait. Sent by God. The other was going to Zach's appearance on television and was so happy to go.

"I will meet up with you later in the Celestial City. I want to hear your good report, and I will tell you mine," one of the angels said to the other. Then, in the speed of thought-like rays of light, they were gone into the glorious mist. They then reappeared instantly at the desired location.

Someday every saint will understand exactly how this works. All the redeemed will be robed in white. They will travel the same way to worlds without end.

14

The Green Room

In the green room, the other guests made up of Christian celebrities gathered. Zach was in the upper echelon of the who's-who list in American ministry. God didn't read the list. But most preachers informally had it in the back of their minds. Every one of the guests kind of orbited Zach like the planets do the sun while waiting for the cameras to roll. That night, the planets would be shaken up a little bit in the world of Christian stardom.

Zach had worked so hard to get there. He had worked so hard to stay there. He didn't know the future, but if he had, he would have liked it. The Bible says, in Proverbs 4:18, "But the path of the just is as the shining light, that shineth more and more unto the perfect day." Tonight, Zach thought maybe his ministry was shrinking and ending. It wasn't. It was just beginning.

Most of the other Christian celebrities in the greenroom had started out right. Some were sincere. Others were not. Many loved God. Some were lukewarm. Almost all were exhausted. For some, ministry had just become a business. There is a business side to ministry. When you don't have money, you can't help many people.

But when you love money and spend people, you are in something, but it is not the ministry.

Every person there was deeply loved by God, and all of them liked Zach. Most all of them wished that they had a so-called ministry like him. A few minutes of his time could be life changing. Just to talk to Zach was a boost to people's ego. They could brag about it to their friends. But inside, not many of them liked each other. And not many of them trusted each other.

These people did not have and honor covenant relationships. They would stab anyone in the back to get ahead. But God's favor would have lifted all of them out of Christian politics. Grace had lifted Zach. He in turn would help many of them to become free.

On air, Zach listened to the other guests joke and laugh. Nervous energy from prayerless people filled the stage. Lighthearted discussion with scarcely a mention of the Savior. Then someone said, "Bro. Zach Whitman. So *great* to have you here tonight. What's been happening in your life?" The host asked the question, but the host sure was not expecting the answer.

Tara sat right beside Zach. Tara put her hand on Zach's arm, squeezed it a little and looked up and smiled at him. It was something that hadn't happened very much the last few years. A smile of respect. There would be countless more of them for Zach in the decades ahead. And on a glorious day, by a heavenly throne, there would be another smile and a voice saying, "Well done."

But on this day, the red light on the camera was pointed right at Zach, and he could scarcely speak. This was a professional speaker who, for

many years, could tame any camera and domi-
nate any television set.

With a broken spirit and a contrite heart,
Zach slowly began to speak:

*"I've asked God and Tara to forgive me for being
hard and indifferent. I've worked so hard to lift up my
name instead of the Lord Jesus Christ. I've been busy,
and tired, and cold in my soul for a long, long time."*

The audience let out a collective gasp of air.
Deathly silence hung in the studio like a thick
smog. The host and the other guests on camera
started to fidget around very uncomfortably.
And Zach just kept talking.

Some people in the audience also began to
fidget. Actually, the word "squirm" in the
Webster's Dictionary might be a better way to
describe it—especially the host and the other
guests. But right then, Zach sensed it. Something

that he had not sensed in a long while.

The anointing.

And with it came an authority and strength that only the Holy Spirit gives when someone is lifting up the name of Jesus. The power to be a witness came upon him.

Other national ministry leaders in their homes began to call each other: "Are you watching? Turn on the Christian TV network." Many laughed because competition and jealousy at that time ran rampant among many ministries. It was a fact. Howls of gleeful laughter permeated a lot of places as Zach poured out his soul.

People that had never liked him liked him even less. It looked like the end. But when you run out of self and run into God, it is never the end. It is always just the beginning.

Deciding that you want peace more than you want a "big ministry" is a sign that God may be getting ready to really use you. Right then, Zach wanted the peace that only Jesus brings more than anything in his life. And then the anointing began to spread. That is the way the Spirit of God moves. From empty vessel to empty vessel. There were a lot of empty vessels there that night.

Guests on the set began to cry. Some just turned around in their chairs and knelt in prayer on national TV. Then God's presence swept into the audience. It went out the doors of the studio. That presence of Jesus saturated every cable and satellite system that it touched. Lukewarm ministers hung their heads and went from mockery to admiration.

Nothing is more exhausting than performing the Gospel in the strength of the flesh when you should be flowing in the *Holy Spirit*. It will make you old. It will make you bitter. It will make you mean. And it does not accomplish the eternal. This was not a performance for Zach. It was not an angle that he was playing to get attention. It was a broken spirit and a contrite heart. And it was real.

"I'm taking three months off to pray and spend with Tara. My most important ministry is at home. If you really love me, pray for me. If I have hurt you, please forgive me." Then Zach prayed, hugged Tara, and they both walked off the set. Tara looked at him with something different in her eyes; it was respect.

That night wasn't the end of anything. It was just the beginning. A lot of old things had passed away. A lot of things inside Zach Whitman's heart had become new. Something else happened that night: angels at the speed of celestial light entered the Holy City. Angels rejoiced. A roar that sounded like the sound of many waters went in wave after wave toward the throne.

An angel found Zach's fifth grade Sunday School, teacher Sis. Coffin. The angel had never spoken to her about Zach before. There had never been anything to tell that would impress Heaven. But the angel robed in white began to glow. Almost transfigured like Jesus before her. And in a transparent scene across the angel's powerful body, Sis. Coffin could see in Heaven what had just happened on Earth. And Heaven rejoiced. And that night Zach rested. Really rested, in Tara's arms and in the arms of Jesus.

15

The Ringside Evangelist

The next few months, Zach fell in love all over again with Jesus, and also fell in love all over again with Tara. Long walks and long talks were the order of the day.

His children actually started liking him and wanting to spend time with him. A new sentence became part of the vocabulary at the Whitman house. It was "where is Dad?" because they all wanted to be together. Anything that they enjoyed was more fun if Dad was there. And anything that Dad enjoyed was more enjoyable if his wife and kids were there.

You see, Zach went from being a preoccupied, selfish man to being a godly dad. He went from being a success in the world's eyes to being a little boy and little girl's hero. This was the greatest ministry he had ever had and ever would have.

Yes, Zach fell in love with Jesus and he fell in love with his wife, Tara, all over again. He even resurrected several old nicknames that he called her: Tara-dactyle, Tara-fin, and Taddie, his personal favorite. Hers too. Names that Zach had called her in high school when they first fell in love.

Two new sounds came to their house. The sound of prayer and laughter. No one had heard those sounds in years. The deafening silence in their home never did come back. Zach's children never thought about what Dad did. About how big his ministry was. They never saw him under pressure, never thought he was too important or too busy to spend time with them. He wasn't. He never would be again. Their children just liked being around him. So did Tara. Every day he spent time with Jesus and spent time with Tara. The more he loved the one, the more he loved the other.

Zach had been prepared to downsize and cut, and go it alone in his new found faith. But his partners loved him for his truthfulness. Mercy found him. There was a realness about Zach that was changing the world. His ministry went to a whole new stratosphere. The whole

Christian world sought after Zach but Zach sought after the Lord. Not money. Not fame. Not success. But the Lord.

The Blessing of the Lord that maketh rich and adds no sorrow came upon him (Proverbs 10:22). It came upon him strong. The Blessing that only God can give. The kind that the world can't take away.

One day when Zach would go to Heaven, the Lord would say, "Well done, Zach." And Zach would be robed in white. And have a new name. And the apostles would seek Zach out. They would want to talk to him because Zach had been such a strategic part of that last *revival*. The *revival* that ushered in the second coming of the Lord Jesus Christ. Zach would live to see the day when the latter rain and the former rain were poured out in one day. The day when the

Gospel was preached in all the world. When God poured His Spirit out on all flesh.

Zach loved Jesus and Jesus loved Zach. And both of them loved Melvin Brankard. Zach reprinted all of the old man's books, and they sold by the tens of thousands. A whole new generation fell in love with the Christ that M. L. Brankard preached.

A thousand Gospel ships launched and answered *the Call to preach* because of what they heard in Melvin Brankard's voice. Gospel ships that sailed and never turned back. Gospel ships that went all over the world carrying the good news that Jesus is the *Savior, Healer, Baptizer, and Soon Coming King.*

And there was another ship that God's grace and Melvin Brankard kept from sinking: the ship of Zach Whitman. It never would sink because

Jesus was now on board.

Yes, Evangelist Brankard never changed but he did change the world. And he changed the world of a desperate, dry preacher named Zach Whitman. A lot can happen in a midweek service with thirty-five people.

Zach bought Evangelist Melvin a house. He bought him a car. Zach bought him a dog. The young evangelist paid a driver to drive Bro. Brankard everywhere he had to go. And go he did. Invitations by the hundreds lay in stacks on the old man's desk.

Dozens of evangelists got started by Jesus and Bro. Melvin. Here are how the phone conversations nearly always went between Bro. Melvin and pastors:

"Now Pastor—yes, I know that you want me to come. And I may come for the last night, as the Lord leads. But Pastor, I've laid hands on this unknown young man and anointed him with oil. I want you to have him. Now take a step of faith, Pastor. And if you don't have him, you are not having me." And the doors swung open for a new wave of evangelists that changed America and impacted the whole world.

Nothing had been seen like it since John Wesley and other believers released circuit riding preachers all over the nation. Now young evangelists, unknown to man but known to God and Bro. Melvin Brankard, hit the highways. The more they preached, the more doors opened for them to preach. And seed brings forth after its own kind. The Called ones helped many more answer the Call into the work of the Lord.

Mighty women of God were Called and preached powerfully. The Gifts and Calling of

God are neither male nor female and know no racial or religious boundaries (Galatians 3:28). And the fading, setting sun on the dispensation of grace stood still because the Lord of the harvest desired that none should perish. but that all men should come to repentance and to a saving knowledge of the Lord Jesus Christ.

Yes, every day Zach talked to Jesus. And nearly every day he talked to Melvin Brankard. In a gravelly voice the old man would say, "Stay small, Zach. Stay small—so Jesus can use you BIG." And Zach listened.

A father never loved his son as much as Evangelist Melvin loved his son in the Lord, Zach. And a boy never loved his dad as much as Zach loved his father in the Lord, Melvin Brankard.

Sometimes in the crusades, if you know

where to look, you can see him. On the front row, a little to the left of center stage. A white-haired, distinguished-looking old man sitting there with tears streaming down his lined face, listening to a handsome young man who also has tears streaming down his face. The evangelist up front once in a while looks down where the old evangelist sits. You can see it if you know what you are looking for. The man on stage is lifting up Jesus, the one that they both love and adore.

The old evangelist is unseen in the crowd but still noticed and talked about in Heaven. Angels will soon come for him in the Rapture or at his beautiful home. But not yet. This week, the old evangelist will preach a few thousand times. He will preach through *the voices* of all the other preachers that he has touched because a part of him that Jesus anointed is on the inside of each of them. But maybe the one he touched the most is Zach. The prodigal who came back to father's house. The rich young ruler who turned out alright. Like an old prizefighter sitting ringside, Bro. Melvin watches Zach punch the devil in the face. He sways side to side while the Gospel punches are thrown. He knows what it is like to be in the ring. He has stood inside the arena. The old man is in the young man's corner. The old man has dreams and the young man has visions. And the visions of the young man are fulfilling the dreams of the old man.

Because Jesus has already won, Zach wins every time. The devil loses every time. Now the young evangelist has God's blessing on every stage, wherever and whenever he preaches. A worldwide stage lifting up JESUS CHRIST. It's the story of THE EVANGELIST. A story of two preachers.

Pray this prayer to ask Jesus into your heart and be saved for all of eternity:

Heavenly Father, in Jesus' name, please forgive me for all of my sin. I believe that You are the true Son of God, and I claim Your shed blood on the cross of Calvary to pay for my sins. Wash me clean from all of my sins, and I will serve You the rest of my life. One day, I want to go to Heaven and live with You forever.

Made in the USA
Middletown, DE
03 April 2021